HUMMINGBIRD

LIVING THINGS

HUMMINGBIRD

Rebecca Stefoff

BENCHMARK BOOKS

MARSHALL CAVENDISH
NEW YORK

Benchmark Books
Marshall Cavendish Corporation
99 White Plains Road
Tarrytown, New York 10591

Illustrations by Jean Cassels

Library of Congress Cataloging-in-Publication Data
Stefoff, Rebecca
Hummingbird / Rebecca Stefoff.
p.   cm. — (Living things)
Includes bibliographical references and index.
Summary: Examines the physical characteristics, life cycle,
and natural habitat of various kinds of hummingbirds.
ISBN 0-7614-0415-5 (lib. bdg.)
1 Hummingbirds—Juvenile literature. [1. Hummingbirds.]
I.Title. II. Series: Stefoff, Rebecca   Living things.
QL696.A558S72   1997   598.7'64—dc21   96-44018   CIP   AC

Photo research by Ellen Barrett Dudley

Cover photo: *The National Audubon Society Collection, Photo Researchers, Inc.*,
Robert Lee

The photographs in this book are used by permission and through the courtesy of:
The National Audubon Society Collection, Photo Researchers, Inc.: Harold
Hungerford, 2; Anthony Mercieca, 6-7, 22; S.C. Fried, 7, 20 (right); Doug Plummer,
8 (left); Bob & Elsie Boggs, 8 (right); Paul Bonino, 9; Leonard Lee Rue, 10; Richard
R. Hansen, 11; John S. Dunning, 14 (right); Jany Sauvanet, 16; Nick Bergkessel, 18,
18-19, 19; Joseph Van Wormer, 23; Jan Lindblad, 26; Francois Gohier, 27. *Animals
Animals*: Michael Fogden, 12, 14 (left), 16-17, 25 (right); Peter Weiman, 15;
Alan G. Nelson, 17; Don Enger, 25 (left); M.A. Chappell, 32. *Peter Arnold, Inc.*:
S.J. Krasemann, 20 (left); Luiz C. Marigo, 21; Russel C. Hansen, 24.

Printed in the United States of America

1   3   5   6   4   2

For Soren

broad-billed hummingbird, Arizona

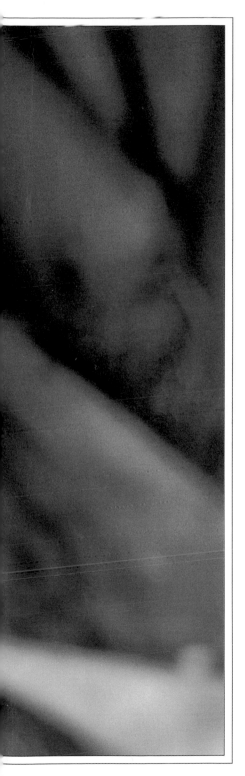

What is this tiny bundle of shiny feathers? It's a hummingbird.

Hummingbirds got their name because of the noise they make when they fly. Their wings move so fast that they give off a humming sound.

Most hummingbirds are little. The world's smallest bird is the bee hummingbird. It's not very much bigger than a honeybee. The hum of its wings sounds like a buzzing bee.

7

The hummingbird starts life as an egg in a small nest. The nest is built of bits of sticks and leaves. The mother bird lines the nest with spiderweb and thistledown to make it soft and warm. Then she keeps her eggs even warmer by sitting on the nest. When the eggs hatch, the mother bird flies back and forth all day, bringing food to the hungry baby birds.

young broad-billed hummingbirds

Baby hummingbirds grow fast. Soon the young birds have a full coat of feathers. When they start flapping their wings, they're ready to learn to fly.

The first trip out of the nest is a big adventure for a little hummingbird. One youngster watches from inside the nest while the other perches on a branch for the first time. Before long, both birds will fly away from the nest to live on their own.

young Anna's hummingbirds

snowcap hummingbird, Costa Rica

Why do we almost always see hummingbirds around flowers?

Hummingbirds live on nectar, the sugary juice inside flowers. They buzz from flower to flower, sipping at the nectar. They especially like red flowers. That's why people who want to see hummingbirds in their gardens plant bushes with red blossoms.

If you see a hummingbird, it will be perching or flying. Its legs are too small and weak to walk, but its strong wings can carry it to more than two hundred flowers in one day.

How does a hummingbird get the nectar out of a flower? By using its pointed beak. Many hummingbirds have specially shaped beaks to help them reach the nectar.

The sicklebill's beak curves far down into a half-

circle. The sicklebill uses this curved beak to poke into skinny flowers that point upward. Other hummingbirds have long straight beaks to reach inside very large flowers. Even a giant banana blossom is not too big for a hungry hummingbird.

long-tailed hermit at hibiscus flower

bronze-tailed plumeteer, Costa Rica

calliope hummingbird, Montana

The hummingbird has a long, thin tongue—even longer than its beak. After the hummingbird sticks its beak into a flower, it uses its tongue to lick up drops of nectar.

It takes a lot of energy for hummingbirds to flap those little wings all day long. To stay strong enough to fly, hummingbirds have to eat a lot. They spend the whole day searching for nectar.

A ruby-throated hummingbird approaches a trumpet creeper blossom . . .   *flies into the flower . . .*

Hummingbirds can do something that no other birds can do. They can fly backward.

For a long time scientists thought no bird could fly backward. "It's impossible!" they said. Then someone

and backs out.

took a closer look. Now we know that these little birds really do fly backward. They fly forward into flowers and then back out again. They can also fly straight up and straight down, like little feathered helicopters.

Hummingbirds are found only in the Americas. Different kinds of hummingbirds make their homes in different places. Some live in pine woodlands. Others make their homes in meadows with lots of bushes and wildflowers.

ruby-throated hummingbird

blue-chinned sapphire hummingbird

Chilean woodstar

If you really want to see a lot of hummingbirds, you'll have to go to the tropical rain forests of Central and South America. More kinds of hummingbirds live there than anywhere else.

giant hummingbird, Peru

Not all hummingbirds are tiny. The bird on this page is the world's largest hummingbird. It lives in South America and is eight and a half inches long (22 cm) from the tip of its beak to the tip of its tail. The hummingbird on the next page is called a streamertail because its blue tail feathers stream out behind it when it flies. The tail is a lot longer than the rest of the bird!

streamertail, Jamaica

male ruby-throated hummingbird

See the beautiful red and green hummingbird
on this page? The red patch on its throat is called
a gorget. Most male hummingbirds have bright-
colored gorgets. The male birds wear brilliant, shiny
colors. The female birds wear softer colors and
don't have gorgets.

Look at the two birds on
this page. Can you guess
which one is a female and
which is a male?

male crowned wood nymph, Costa Rica

female ruby-throated hummingbird

rufous-breasted hermit building nest

New life begins when a mother hummingbird gathers leaves, grass, and spiderweb to make a nest. Then she lays her eggs. Sitting on the nest, she is almost invisible in the trees. But if you look closely you can see a bright, shiny green speck of life, like a jewel with feathers—a hummingbird.

rufous-tailed hummingbird

A QUICK LOOK AT THE HUMMINGBIRD

Hummingbirds are found only in North, Central, and South America. There are 341 different kinds, or species, of hummingbirds. They live in forests, meadows, and brushy grasslands from Chile and Argentina in the south to Canada in the north. The greatest number of species is found in the tropical regions.

Here are six kinds of hummingbirds along with their scientific names in Latin and a few key facts.

BEE HUMMINGBIRD

Mellisuga helenae
[meh lih SOO gah HEH leh nye]
Smallest of all hummingbirds and also world's smallest bird at two inches long. Weighs less than a penny. Eggs are one-third of an inch across. Lives in Cuba. Is becoming rare and may soon be an endangered species.

RUBY-THROATED HUMMINGBIRD

Archilochus colubris
[ar kih LOH cus coh LOO bris]
The only hummingbird that lives in North America east of the Rocky Mountains. Often seen in gardens and at edges of woodlands. Measures about 4 inches (10 cm) in length.

WHITE-CRESTED COQUETTE

Lophornis adorabilis
[loh FOR nis ah dor ah BEE lis]
A small, plump hummingbird, about
3 inches (8 cm) long, with short bill and tail.
Has crests or tufts of feathers on head. Lives only in
Costa Rica.

RUFOUS HUMMINGBIRD

Selasphorus rufus
[seh LASS foh rus ROO fus]
Named for its color—"rufous" means
"reddish." Measures 4 inches (10 cm) in
length. Lives in western North America,
mostly in Pacific Northwest, British
Columbia, and southern Alaska. Found in
mountain forests in the fall and lowland
forests in the spring.

WHITE-TIPPED SICKLEBILL

Eutoxeres aquilia
[you TOH zeh rez ah KWIH lee ah]
Measures about 5 inches (13 cm)in length.
Name comes from white tips on tail feathers
and bill that is curved like a sickle (a blade for
cutting wheat). Uses bill to probe downward inside
narrow flowers. Lives in Central and South America,
from Costa Rica to Ecuador.

GIANT HUMMINGBIRD

Patagona gigas

[pah tah GOH nah GUY gahs]

World's largest hummingbird. Measures 8-1/2 inches (22 cm) in length. Lives in the Andes Mountains of South America, in Chile, Peru, and Ecuador.

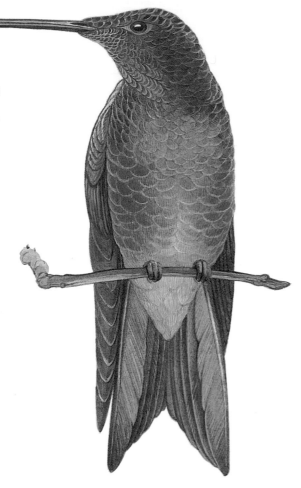

Taking Care of the Hummingbird

Some kinds of hummingbirds are becoming rare as the forests where they live are cut down. Saving woodlands throughout the Americas will help give hummingbirds a home for the future. Many kinds of hummingbirds can also live in parks and suburban areas with gardens. You can attract hummingbirds to your home by planting flowering bushes, or you can buy a special hummingbird feeder at a garden store. Hummingbirds help plants reproduce by spreading pollen as they fly from flower to flower.

Find Out More

Gans, Roma. *Hummingbirds in the Garden*. New York: Crowell, 1969.

Hummingbirds up Close. (Video) Carrboro, N.C.: Nature Science Network, 1988.

Simon, Hilda. *Wonders of Hummingbirds*. New York: Dodd, Mead, 1964.

Tyrrell, Esther Quesada. *Hummingbirds: Jewels in the Sky*. New York: Crown, 1992.

Index

Rebecca Stefoff has published many books for young readers. Science and environmental issues are among her favorite subjects. She lives in Oregon and enjoys observing the natural world while hiking, camping, and scuba diving.

young Anna's hummingbirds in nest